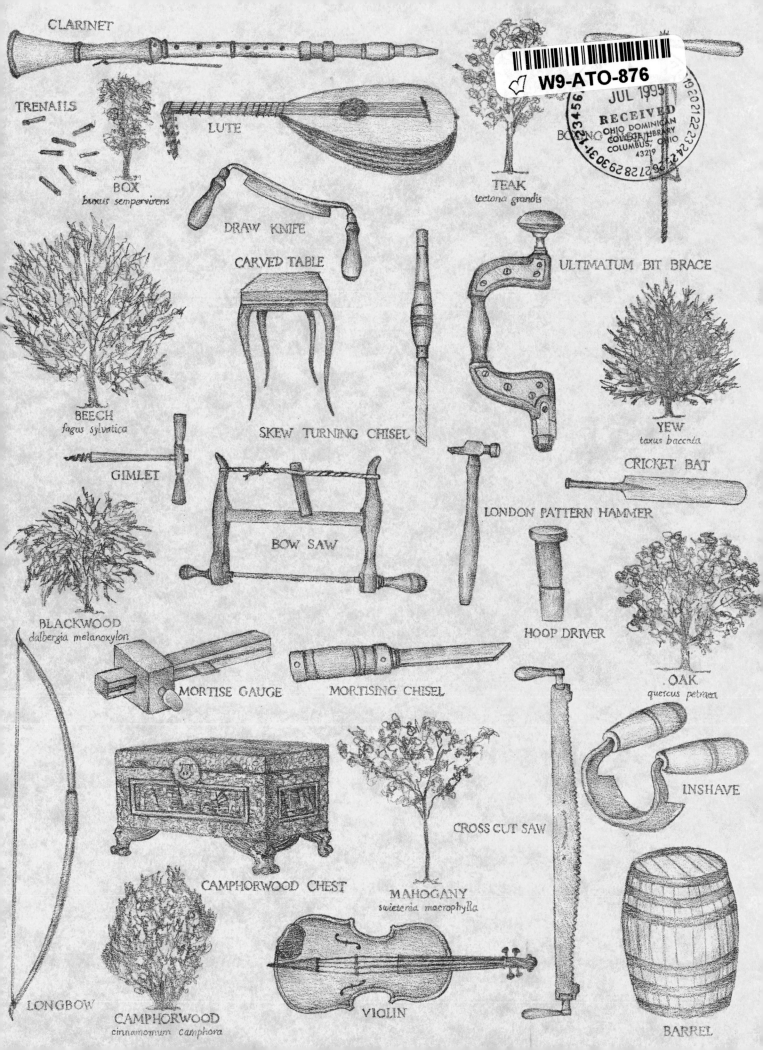

CLARINET

TRENAILS

LUTE

BOX
buxus sempervirens

TEAK
tectona grandis

DRAW KNIFE

CARVED TABLE

ULTIMATUM BIT BRACE

BEECH
fagus sylvatica

SKEW TURNING CHISEL

YEW
taxus baccata

GIMLET

CRICKET BAT

BOW SAW

LONDON PATTERN HAMMER

BLACKWOOD
dalbergia melanoxylon

HOOP DRIVER

MORTISE GAUGE

MORTISING CHISEL

OAK
quercus petraea

INSHAVE

CROSS CUT SAW

CAMPHORWOOD CHEST

MAHOGANY
swietenia macrophylla

LONGBOW

CAMPHORWOOD
cinnamomum camphora

VIOLIN

BARREL

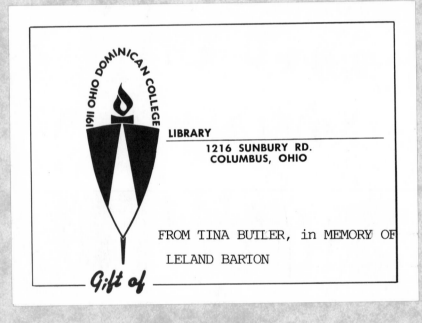

WOODLORE

CAMERON MILLER
and DOMINIQUE FALLA

Ticknor & Fields Books for Young Readers
New York 1995

Dominique Falla did the illustrations for this book on plywood
primed with Gesso, using aquarelles (water-soluble pencils).
Cameron Miller framed each illustration with the actual wood
described in the text and used a variety of other timbers
for the inlay work and decorations.

◆

Copyright © 1994 by Cameron Miller and Dominique Falla

First American edition 1995 published by
Ticknor & Fields Books for Young Readers
A Houghton Mifflin company, 215 Park Avenue South,
New York, New York 10003.

First published in Australia by Omnibus Books

Manufactured in the United States of America
Typography by David Saylor
The text of this book is set in 22 point Goudy Bold

BVG 10 9 8 7 6 5 4 3 2 1

LIBRARY OF CONGRESS CATALOGING-IN-PUBLICATION DATA
Miller, Cameron.
Woodlore / by Cameron Miller and Dominique Falla.
—1st American ed.   p. cm.   ISBN 0-395-72034-6
1. Woodwork—Juvenile literature. 2. Wood—Juvenile literature.
[1. Woodwork. 2. Wood.] I. Falla, Dominique. II. Title.
TT185.M47 1995 674'.8—dc20
94-27987 CIP AC

Thanks, Eddy!

Yew trees,
grown throughout the ages,
Have the wood
the bowyer favors.

Maple and spruce
are always kings
For makers of lutes
and violins.

Bodgers made the
Windsor chair
From beechwood,
turned and left to air.

Alder wood is cut into logs,
Seasoned, tapered, and carved
into clogs.

For furniture fit for royalty
The New World gave mahogany.

Blackwood and box are
hard and dense
To make sweet woodwind
instruments.

Ash felloes are best, the wheelwrights say,
Cut from boughs that bend the right way.

The use of cherry and
walnut defines
The simple beauty
of Shaker designs.

When ships sailed out from dock to trade,
Of Burmese teak the decks were made.

Traditionally,
yellow pine, of course,
Makes the perfect
rocking horse.

Oak flitches are what
the cooper saves.
He makes them into
barrel staves.

A camphorwood chest
for clothes, they say,
Keeps moths and
silverfish away.

Young willow trees that grow in glades
Are split into wedges for cricket bat blades.

Notes on Illustrations

Yew The longbow was first developed by the Welsh, who used it with great success in battle against the English in the thirteenth century. Longbows were later used extensively throughout Britain and Europe until firearms were invented. The bowyer preferred to make the bow from a single piece of yew, using both the harder heartwood (for strength) and the sapwood (for flexibility). The illustration on the left-hand page shows a bowyer in medieval times making a longbow with basic hand tools; the right-hand page shows men using their bows in target practice. Yew trees were often planted in churchyards, where, according to superstition, they kept evil spirits away.

Maple and Spruce The famous violin-maker Antonio Stradivari lived in the seventeenth century in the Italian town of Cremona, at that time the violin capital of the world. The illustrations show the front and interior of a typical Italian instrument-maker's workshop, where a craftsman is working on a child's violin. The back of a violin is usually carved from maple and the belly from the softer spruce. The design of the "f" holes in the belly varies from maker to maker, like a signature. The lute, a much older instrument, has a curved back made of maple ribs. It was introduced to Europe from Arabia in the thirteenth century, but by the seventeenth century it was becoming less popular.

Beech Bodgers were craftsmen who went out into the beech forests of England to make the legs and spindles for Windsor chairs. They first split the beechwood into logs and then shaped the logs roughly on a shave horse, as shown in the foreground of the left-hand illustration. The resulting "blanks" were shaped and turned (rounded) on a pole lathe, and the finished spindles were sold to a chair-maker (shown in the right-hand illustration), who constructed the complete chair. "Windsor" describes a style of country chair in which the back section and the legs are fitted separately to the top and underside of the seat. The name was first recorded in 1724.

Alder Clogs—work shoes made entirely of wood—were popular for centuries in northern European countries, and water-resistant alderwood was traditionally used for their manufacture. Like bodgers, cloggers would set up camp in an alder grove where they worked for months at a time. First they split the timber into rough clog shapes, and then they piled them into conical stacks to allow the wood to dry out, or "season." Later they shaped the outside of the clogs with a stock knife and hollowed out the inside with gouges, and finally the clogs would be shaped to fit the individual wearer's feet. The illustration shows eighteenth-century French cloggers at work.

Mahogany

These illustrations show scenes from around 1770, a period when the great English craftsmen Chippendale, Hepplewhite, and Sheraton designed styles of furniture that are still valued and copied today. Mahogany, introduced to European countries from Central and South America in the seventeenth century, is an ideal timber for furniture-making. Its close grain allows it to be carved in intricate detail; it can be tapered to make slender, elegant pieces that are both strong and light; and it can be highly polished. The left-hand illustration shows cabinetmakers working at their benches; at right a richly dressed woman is shown in a room containing beautiful mahogany furniture—which, in those days, only the wealthy could afford.

Blackwood and Box

During the seventeenth and eighteenth centuries, before the time of large symphony orchestras, woodwind instruments such as the clarinet, flute, oboe, and bassoon were played mainly by small groups who performed chamber music and church music. All such instruments were handmade, constructed from short, hollow sections of wood that fitted snugly together. The sections were turned on a lathe, as shown in the left-hand illustration, and the finger holes were bored in

later. Instrument-makers selected their woods very carefully. Both blackwood and box are dense timbers that turn well, without splitting, and allow a good, even musical tone.

Ash

The center of a wooden wheel, known as the hub or nave, is usually made of hard-wearing elm wood, and the spokes that radiate from the hub are made of oak that is split instead of sawed, to preserve the strength of the timber. The felloes are the curved sections that form the rim of the wheel, and for these the best timber to use is ash, a shock-resistant timber that can safely absorb all the jolting and pounding a wheel must withstand. The wheel is held together with an iron hoop tire. A blacksmith heats the metal and hammers it over the rim, then cools it with water so that as it contracts, it jams the wheel tightly together. The illustration shows a typical wheelwright's shop in the early nineteenth century.

Cherry and Walnut

The Shakers, a religious community founded in the United States in 1774, have long been renowned for their skill in making domestic articles and furniture. In keeping with their belief in simplicity and purity, everything they made was beautiful but functional, without decoration and often unpainted. For storage and easy cleaning, chairs, tables, mirrors, clocks, brooms, and candleholders were hung on peg boards that lined every room. The Shakers were famous for their oval boxes with the distinctive "swallowtail" joint holding the flexible sides together—shown here in the border around the illustrations. The Shaker motto was "Hands to work, hearts to God."

Teak In the eighteenth and nineteenth centuries the decks of most sailing ships were made from teak because it contains an oil that is especially resistant to water. Most of the teak came from Burma or India. Ship decking was constructed from long planks nailed down to crossbeams with round oak pegs called trenails. Oakum (fiber from old rope) was forced into the seams between the planks to make the deck watertight, and tar or pitch was then used to fill the seams and make the surface hard-wearing.

Yellow Pine The rocking horse reached the height of its popularity in the nineteenth century. The model horse was fixed at the hoofs to curved runners or to a hinged frame, allowing a child mounted on the horse to rock backward and forward. Yellow pine was commonly used for making this sort of toy because it is soft and can be carved easily, although the horse's legs and the runners were often made from a stronger timber, such as beechwood. The illustration on the left-hand page shows the toymaker carving the head of a horse from blocks of wood that have been glued together.

Oak Barrel-making is a very ancient craft: in Egypt, barrels were used as early as 2600 B.C. The illustration on the left shows two barrel-makers, or coopers, at work in a nineteenth-century workshop. Using a drawknife, the cooper shapes oak flitches (split pieces of timber) into tapered strips of wood called staves, which are held together by iron hoops. A circular top and bottom, also of oak, are fitted into grooves inside the staves. The rounded shape of the barrel makes it easy to move and stack, even when it is full. Barrels are most often used as containers for wine or beer, and some large breweries and wineries still employ their own coopers. The right-hand illustration shows a draft-horse pulling a brewer's cart.

Camphorwood Camphorwood is the popular name given to the fragrant timber of the camphor laurel, a tree native to Japan, Taiwan and China, but now also found in many other countries. Ornate chests made from this timber have long been used for storing clothes, as the scent is said to repel moths and silverfish, which feed on woolen clothes. The first such chests came from China. The lid and sides were intricately carved with oriental scenes of trade, travel, and daily life, and the timber was finished with the dark, shiny lacquer much used in Chinese woodwork. The chests were exported around the world and are still made and used today.

Willow Cricket is a ball game that originated in England. The earliest cricket bats were made in the seventeenth century and were curved and almost twice as heavy as modern bats. Bats were not made with a separate blade and handle until the mid-nineteenth century; by 1900, the design seen in the illustration was well established. The bat's handle, made from alternate strips of cane and gutta-percha (a rubbery substance), and bound together with string or rubber, was spliced into the blade of compressed and shaped willow wood. Unlike baseball bats, which are made from ash, the best cricket bats were said to be made from quick-growing willow trees planted on riverbanks: the resilience and pliability of this wood made it capable of absorbing the powerful impact of a cricket ball.